My First Acrostic

All About Me

Northern Ireland

Edited By Daisy Job

First published in Great Britain in 2019 by:

Young Writers
Remus House
Coltsfoot Drive
Peterborough
PE2 9BF
Telephone: 01733 890066
Website: www.youngwriters.co.uk

Book Design by Ashley Janson

Softback ISBN 978-1-83928-569-1
Hardback ISBN 978-1-83928-570-7
Printed and bound in the UK by BookPrintingUK
Website: www.bookprintinguk.com
YB0426R

Dear Reader,

Dear Reader,

Welcome to a fun-filled book of acrostic poems!

Here at Young Writers, we are delighted to introduce our new poetry competition for KS1 pupils, *My First Acrostic: All About Me*. Acrostic poems are an enjoyable way to introduce pupils to the world of poetry and allow the young writer to open their imagination to a range of topics of their choice. The colourful and engaging entry forms allowed even the youngest (or most reluctant) of pupils to create a poem using the acrostic technique, and with that, encouraged them to include other literary techniques such as similes and description. Here at Young Writers we are passionate about introducing the love and art of creative writing to the next generation and we love being a part of their journey.

From pets to family, from hobbies to idols, these pupils have shaped and crafted their ideas brilliantly, showcasing their budding creativity. So, we invite you to proceed through these pages and take a glimpse into these blossoming young writers' minds. We hope you will relish these poems as much as we have.

Contents

The Poems

Luca-Benny

L uca is my name.
U pstairs on my PS2.
C ool boy.
A lvin is my favourite.
-
B rilliant boy.
E ggs are my favourite healthy food.
N ovember is my birthday.
N ever crazy.
Y awn is what I want to do at night-time.

Luca-Benny Fitzpatrick (6)
Enniskillen Integrated Primary School, Drumcoo

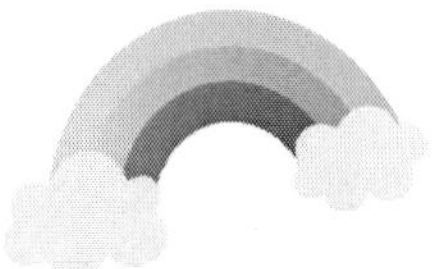

Bethany

B eautiful Bethany.
E lephants are her favourite animal.
T ries her best.
H er hair is long and shiny.
A pples are her favourite fruit.
N utella is her favourite thing to put on her toast.
Y esterday, she worked hard.

Bethany Carty (6)
Enniskillen Integrated Primary School, Drumcoo

Alexander

A lexander is my name.
L ooking cool.
E veryone likes me.
E **X** cellent artist.
A wesome at building.
N umber work is good fortune.
D inosaurs are cool.
E xplorer.
R eading is my favourite.

Alexander Patmalnieks (7)
Enniskillen Integrated Primary School, Drumcoo

Harrison Liggett

H arrison is my name.
A pples are my favourite food.
R eading is my hobby.
R obin is my favourite film.
I ce cream is my favourite.
S uper strong.
O ranges are my favourite fruit.
N ever sad.

Harrison Liggett (6)
Enniskillen Integrated Primary School, Drumcoo

Mohamed

M y name is Mohammed.
O utside, I love to play.
H aving a good time at school.
A pples are my favourite fruit.
M y favourite superhero is Spider-Man.
E very day, I work hard.
D ancing is fun.

Mohamed Fadul (7)
Enniskillen Integrated Primary School, Drumcoo

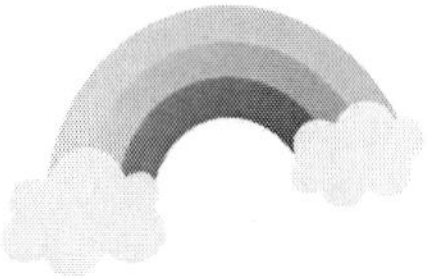

Charlie

C harlie is my name.
H urley is fun.
A t football every day.
R eally loves football.
L ove swimming.
I t was time for tennis.
E verything is good with Charlie.

Charlie McDonald (6)
Enniskillen Integrated Primary School, Drumcoo

Taylia

T ea is coming and I like it.
A t the park, it is so much fun.
Y ellow is my favourite colour.
L ions roar in the jungle.
I love my dolls.
A ll day, the sun shines.

Taylia Ria McCauley (7)
Enniskillen Integrated Primary School, Drumcoo

Oliver

O liver is my name.
L ions are cool.
I like eating ice cream and chocolate.
V iolins are fun to play.
E lephants are my favourite pet.
R abbits are cute.

Oliver Paton (7)
Enniskillen Integrated Primary School, Drumcoo

Justin

J ustin is my name.
U nselfish at all times.
S uper Justin being kind.
T alents are cool.
'I ncredibles' is an amazing film.
N uts are disgusting.

Justin Johnston (7)
Enniskillen Integrated Primary School, Drumcoo

Darragh

D arragh is my name.
A wesome.
R unning very fast.
R eally good at poetry.
A m really kind.
G ood at football.
H andsome.

Darragh Ryan McLoughlin (7)
Enniskillen Integrated Primary School, Drumcoo

Zinnia

Z innia is my name.
I am good at art.
N othing can hurt me.
N ice to everyone.
I am an ice queen.
A lways plays with everyone.

Zinnia Beeson (6)
Enniskillen Integrated Primary School, Drumcoo

Logan

L eaves are fun to jump in.
O ranges are my favourite.
G rapes are my favourite.
A t the pool, it is fun.
N ectarines are a great fruit.

Logan Burns (6)
Enniskillen Integrated Primary School, Drumcoo

Jessica

J essica is my name.
E xcellent at Jets.
S miling all the time.
S mart.
I am a lovely girl.
C aring.
A wesome.

Jessica Wills (6)
Enniskillen Integrated Primary School, Drumcoo

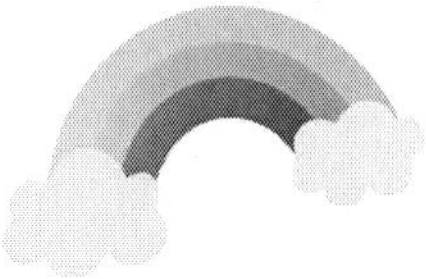

Maddox

M agic.
A mazing boy.
D apper.
D addy and me playing football.
O ne day, I helped my sister tidy her room.
E **X** cellent.

Maddox Walmsley (6)
Enniskillen Integrated Primary School, Drumcoo

James

J ames is my name.
A lex is my best friend.
M y mum and dad are the best.
E very day, I eat bacon.
S trawberries are my favourite.

James Gallagher (6)

Enniskillen Integrated Primary School, Drumcoo

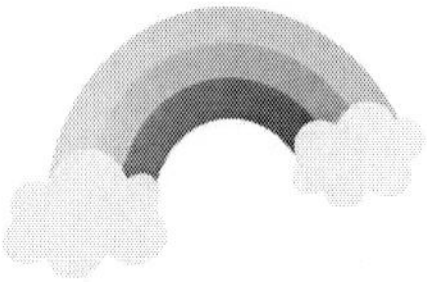

Joseph

J oseph is amazing.
O utside on my bike.
S uper at reading.
E xcellent friending.
P ower is reading.
H opping is fun.

Joseph Harris (7)
Enniskillen Integrated Primary School, Drumcoo

Klavs

K ind and helpful.
L ove my beautiful mother.
A mazing at numbers.
V ery good at making people laugh.
S uper at building Lego.

Klavs Paurnietis
Enniskillen Integrated Primary School, Drumcoo

Cooper

C ool dude.
O ranges are nice.
O utside is fun.
P erfect at running.
E xcellent at work.
R eally good at reading.

Cooper J Love (7)
Enniskillen Integrated Primary School, Drumcoo

Hope

H ome is my favourite place to be.
O ranges are squeezy.
P rincess Hope with a pink crown.
E lephants have long trunks and I like them.

Hope Olivia Black (6)
Enniskillen Integrated Primary School, Drumcoo

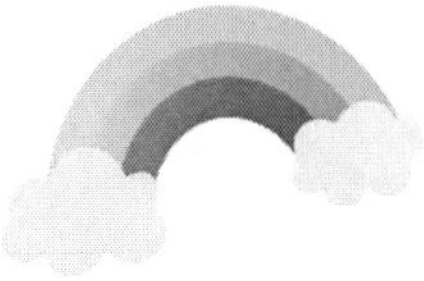

Maggie Francis

M agic manners.
A mazing art.
G reat dreams.
G ood friend.
I nsects are nice.
E very friend of mine is gentle.

Maggie Rose Francis (6)
Enniskillen Integrated Primary School, Drumcoo

Alfie

A mazing at reading in a group.
L ove lemons.
F ire engines are red.
I am a super reader.
E lephants are big.

Alfie Miller (6)
Enniskillen Integrated Primary School, Drumcoo

Ellie

E llie is my name.
L ucky girl.
L ike my friends.
I rish dancing is my favourite.
E ggs on toast, I like them.

Ellie Calderwood (7)
Enniskillen Integrated Primary School, Drumcoo

Filip

F abulous.
I love my brother Nathan.
L ove my mum and dad.
I like playing Minecraft.
P iano is my hobby.

Filip Lucic (7)
Enniskillen Integrated Primary School, Drumcoo

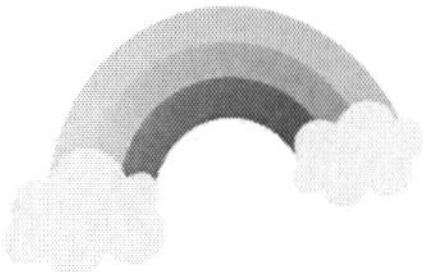

Aoife

A wesome.
O utside, I ride my bike in the commons.
I am good at playing the piano.
F ast running.
E pic.

Aoife Masson (6)
Enniskillen Integrated Primary School, Drumcoo

Ethan

E xcellent at number work.
T errified of spiders.
H opping is fun.
A mazing at maths.
N ice to everyone.

Ethan Judge (6)
Enniskillen Integrated Primary School, Drumcoo

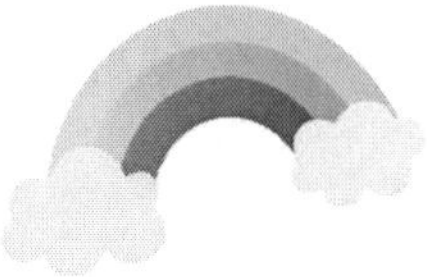

Jake

J umping Jake.
A mazing at reading in my group and like them.
K angaroos jump high.
E veryone plays together.

Jake McManus (6)
Enniskillen Integrated Primary School, Drumcoo

Jake

J umping is fun.
A pples are my favourite fruit.
K eeping the golden rules.
E very Saturday, I watch a film.

Jake Bradley (6)
Enniskillen Integrated Primary School, Drumcoo

David

D avid is my name.
A mazing at reading.
V is in the vowels.
I love swimming.
D igging is fun.

David Ferreira (6)
Enniskillen Integrated Primary School, Drumcoo

Ethan

E than is my name.
T rampolining is fun.
H appy is my favourite game.
A wesome boy.
N ice boy.

Ethan Breen (7)
Enniskillen Integrated Primary School, Drumcoo

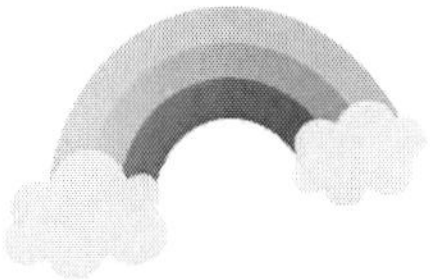

Goda

G ood girl Goda is helpful.
O ranges are my favourite.
D ad gives me candy.
A nimals are my favourite.

Goda Li Markauskaite (6)
Enniskillen Integrated Primary School, Drumcoo

Rachel

R achel is my name.
A mazing at games.
C ool.
H appy.
E pic.
L ovely girl.

Rachel Nixon (6)
Enniskillen Integrated Primary School, Drumcoo

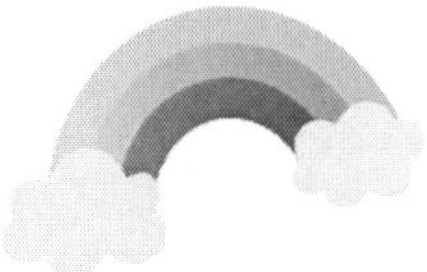

Cody

C olour.
O range is my favourite colour.
D inosaurs are colourful.
Y ellow, red, blue and green.

Cody McMulkin (6)
Enniskillen Integrated Primary School, Drumcoo

Lee

L ee is my name.
E ating Jenny's dinner and desserts,
yummy.
E very day, I like going on my hoverboard.

Lee McCann (6)

Enniskillen Integrated Primary School, Drumcoo

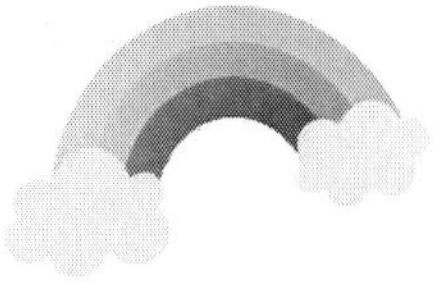

Ellie-May

E njoys running.
L ove my family.
L ego is fun.
I like wildlife.
E xcellent.

Ellie-May Boyd-McManus (6)
Enniskillen Integrated Primary School, Drumcoo

Sean McGullion

S uper at sharing.
E xcellent at being kind.
A good friend to everyone.
N ice to Niall.

Sean James McGullion (6)

Enniskillen Integrated Primary School, Drumcoo

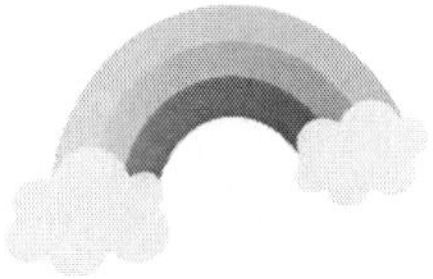

Conrad

C ool boy.
O kay.
N ice.
R ight.
A lright.
D inosaurs are cool.

Conrad Phillip (6)
Enniskillen Integrated Primary School, Drumcoo

Ella

E xcellent at numbers.
L ovely, kind and gentle.
L ong brown hair.
A mazing girl.

Ella Maureen Bernice Neal (7)
Enniskillen Integrated Primary School, Drumcoo

Jory

J umping Jory.
O utside is fun.
R unning is fun.
Y esterday, I worked hard.

Jory Kettyles (6)
Enniskillen Integrated Primary School, Drumcoo

Alex

A lex is my name.
L ee is my friend.
E veryone is my friend.
X box is fun.

Alex Harty (6)
Enniskillen Integrated Primary School, Drumcoo

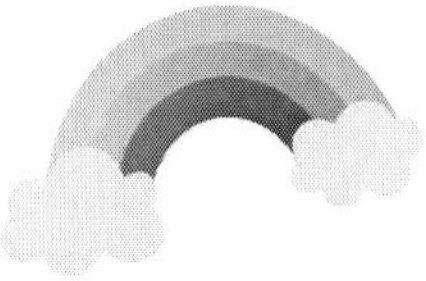

Cian McCauley

C ian is my name.
I am strong.
A wesome.
N ice boy.

Cian McCauley (6)
Enniskillen Integrated Primary School, Drumcoo

Mermaids

M agical creatures under the sea
E legance is a mermaid's type of thing
R esting and relaxing in a clamshell
M ermaids have sparkly scales
A mazing sights under the sea
I n the sea, they have lots of fish friends
D efinitely mermaids have pearls
S hiny seahorses diving into the seaweed.

Jess Barr (7)
Moyle Primary School, Larne

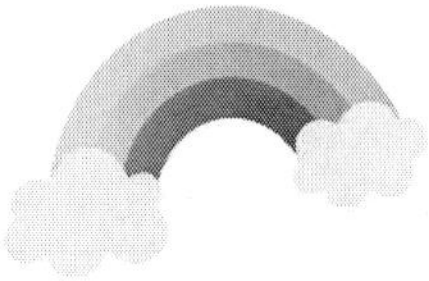

Science

S cience is my favourite subject
C an do experiments and solve problems
I gloos can be found in the Arctic
E lephants can be seen in a zoo
N uts can't be in school because people are allergic
C alculators can be used to solve things
E ating healthy is good for you.

Yumi Ku (8)
Moyle Primary School, Larne

Hamsters

H amsters are always happy when they get food
A nimals that eat a lot of food
M ad runners
S uper creatures
T hey try to climb out their cage so they can be free
E xercise on their wheel a lot
R un a lot through the night
S leep in day, awake at night.

Courtney Harris (7)
Moyle Primary School, Larne

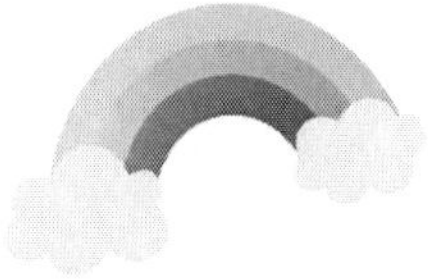

Football

F ood and drinks at half-time
O ut kicking the ball far
O n the football pitch, the players play
T eam players need to be fit to play
B alls going left and right
A lways team discussions
L eap into the goal net
L eap into the crowd.

Luke Savage (7)
Moyle Primary School, Larne

Lanzarote

L ook at the pool
A ll having fun
N othing but ice cream
Z ip up my jumper at night
A eroplane went up in the sky for four hours
R unning to the pool
O utside having a walk
T o the pool I go
E veryone had a good time.

Evie Crofts (7)
Moyle Primary School, Larne

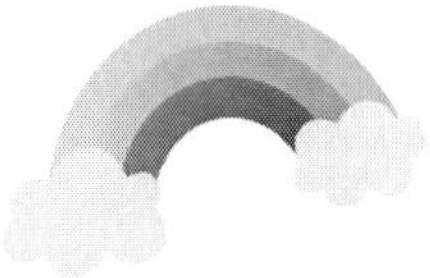

Katie Boyd

K ind and helpful
A lovely person
T aking time to learn
I ce cream is my favourite treat
E nergy to play

B ig and bold
O utside is where I would be
Y oung, beautiful, loving person
D ogs are very loyal to me.

Katie Boyd (7)
Moyle Primary School, Larne

Football

F ootball is very fun
O ut on the move
O ut on your feet
T unes are happy when you score
B alls go everywhere when you kick them
A ctive, makes you run more
L ots of fun at training time
L ots of fun with your training mates.

Gracie Hodge (7)
Moyle Primary School, Larne

Friends

F avourite game is cops and robbers
R un like zombies
I t is not our favourite game
E very day I play with my friends
N uts are not my favourite things to eat
D o we go to the pool on Friday?
S unny day, we go to the park.

Stephen Thomas James King (8)
Moyle Primary School, Larne

Football

F ootball is lots of fun
O ut on the pitch, you can play matches
O n your toes every minute
T unes when someone scores
B alls go everywhere
A ctive on the spot
L ong shots
L ove playing outside.

Kennedy Morrow (7)
Moyle Primary School, Larne

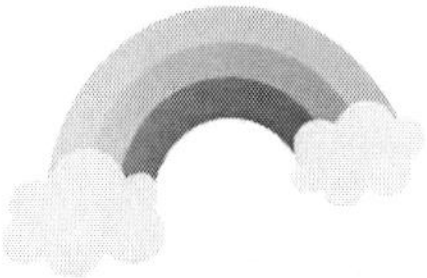

Football

F ootball is very fun
O ut on the go
O n your toes
T unes of celebrations when we score
B alls go everywhere
A lways working as a team
L ots of talk at half-time
L aughter and fun every minute.

Ellie McLean (7)
Moyle Primary School, Larne

Friends

F riday is fun because I call on my friends
R acing you to the house
I like you, friend
E ggs, do you like eggs? I do
N o, I hate nuts
D ad is fun to play with
S aturday is swimming, it is fun.

Chloe Elizabeth Picken (7)
Moyle Primary School, Larne

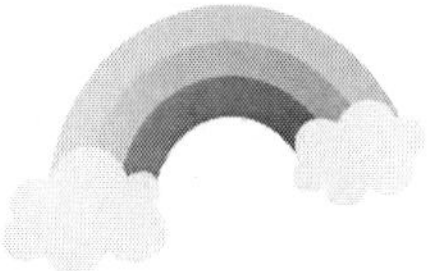

Sophie

S pongeBob is my favourite thing to watch
O range is my favourite colour
P ancakes are my favourite breakfast
H orses are my favourite animal
I ce cream is my favourite treat
E very day I play outside.

Sophie Green-McConnell (7)
Moyle Primary School, Larne

Unicorn

U nicorns live up in the sky
N ose with a horn full of magic
I t has sparkly wings to fly up high
C ute and fluffy
O n the magical clouds
R ainbows are colourful
N ice and kind.

Lauren Rogan (8)
Moyle Primary School, Larne

Mermaid

M ermaids like to swim
E at seaweed
R ainbow colours
M ermaids like to play underwater
A mazing underwater tricks
I n the water, there are pearls
D iving in the water.

Chloe Lomas (7)
Moyle Primary School, Larne

Kitten

K ittens are cute
I n the sun, kittens drink milk
T hey wag their tail when they're happy
T hey are playful and adorable
E nergetic kittens
N o kittens or cats like the rain.

Elliane Saunderson (7)
Moyle Primary School, Larne

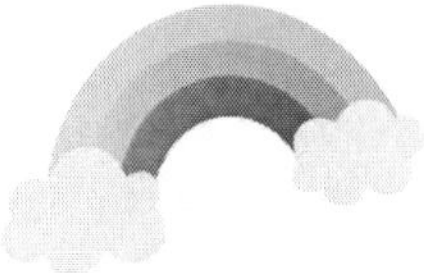

Football

F riends to play with
O utside on the pitch
O n the spot, we run
T alking on the sidelines
B alls on the go
A ctive
L ots of training
L ots of exercise.

Sophia Whelan (8)
Moyle Primary School, Larne

Rabbit

R abbits are small and fluffy
A rabbit is cute
B unny rabbits can hop
B unny rabbits are soft
I love bunny rabbits
T he bunny rabbit has only just been born.

Stacie Ellen Maud Clements (8)
Moyle Primary School, Larne

Forest

F rogs were hopping around
O range is my favourite colour
R ipple ice cream is my favourite
E veryone had fun
S ticks are big
T rees are massive.

James Rowe (7)
Moyle Primary School, Larne

Sloth

S low as can be
L ovely furry sloths relaxing in the sun
O n the tree, having dinner
T iny little babies playing about
H iding when it's time to sleep.

Luci Sofia Brownlee (7)

Moyle Primary School, Larne

Lunch

L unch is my favourite
U nder the stairs, there are sweets
N ear my house, there is a shop
C risps are my favourite food
H ot food is nice.

Lily Graham (7)
Moyle Primary School, Larne

Hotel

H appy holidays at the hotel
O range hotel walls
T Vs in our hotel rooms
E ating such delicious food
L ove the hotel room beds.

Harry Allen (7)
Moyle Primary School, Larne

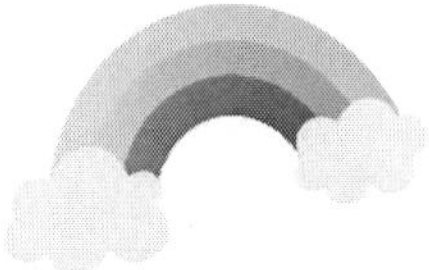

Home

H arry Potter room for hide-and-seek
O rganised all the time and tidy
M ummy, Daddy, me, Ethan and Owen
E nergy to play games together.

Erin Howard (7)
Moyle Primary School, Larne

Rosie

R osie is my dog
O h! I love her
S ometimes I take my dog for a walk
I let Rosie out in the garden
E veryone loves Rosie.

Cassandra Smith (7)
Moyle Primary School, Larne

Spain

S unny weather
P ools to go swimming
A lways hot
I ce cream to keep you cool
N ever-ending slides to slide down.

Mason McConnell (8)
Moyle Primary School, Larne

Spain

S pain is really fun
P arty time is fun
A coconut fell off a tree
I am happy I am here
N uts are delicious.

Jake Wharry (7)

Moyle Primary School, Larne

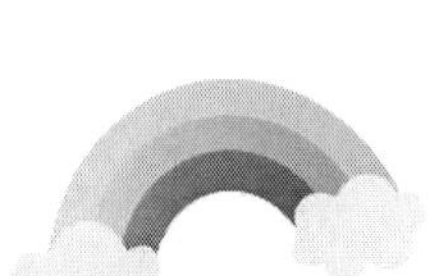

Cats

C ats are cute and fluffy
A nimals that are lazy
T hey can hiss and bite
S ometimes they can be different colours.

Tina Smyth (7)
Moyle Primary School, Larne

Dogs

D ogs drink to keep healthy
O nly good dogs get treats
G ood dogs go for walks
S ome dogs bark!

Ty Snoddy (7)
Moyle Primary School, Larne

Dogs

D rinking water
O utside playing in the backyard
G oing on a walk
S itting on the sofa.

Jayce Steele (7)
Moyle Primary School, Larne

Seal

S wimming all day
E ating and sleeping on the ice
A mazing tricks
L ove the Arctic.

Amelia Ogilvie (7)
Moyle Primary School, Larne

Car

C ars are very fast
A car can go a hundred miles an hour
R unning is far slower than a car.

Charlie McCaw (8)
Moyle Primary School, Larne

Mac

M y cat is my best friend
A cat can attack a bird
C ats are fun.

Harmony McIlwaine (7)
Moyle Primary School, Larne

Granda Clarke

G ardening and flowering was his happy place.
R unning around outside with him, I loved.
A superman he was to me.
N ever cross, always happy.
D ashing and handsome.
A guardian angel he is to me now.

C herishing every memory I have.
L oving, caring, hugging me, I loved
A dventures with him.
R eading and making up stories.
K ind to everyone he was.
E ven made time to dance with me.

Darcy Clarke (5)
Newbuildings Primary School, Londonderry

Unicorn

U p in the sky, they like to fly.
N eigh is the sound they make, just like a horse.
I n the rainbow world is where they live.
C olourful coat and tail.
O ats and apples are what they like to eat.
R ainbow magic helps them fly.
N othing can fly as fast as a unicorn.

Charlotte McClay (5)
Newbuildings Primary School, Londonderry

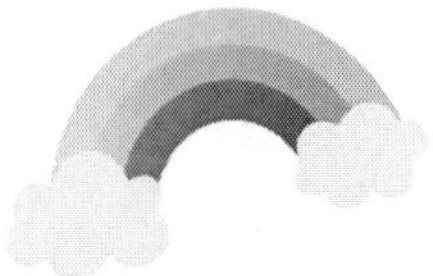

Brandon

B ig and sometimes bad.
R unning around outside.
A lways playing with cars.
N ever sits down.
D on't like sweets.
O range colour, I don't like.
N aughty but lovable.

Brandon Richmond (6)
Newbuildings Primary School, Londonderry

Princesses

P erfect hair.
R egal manner.
I ce-cool.
N ever stressed.
C aring about
E veryone.
S o hopefully
S omeday
E veryone is the
S ame.

Annie-May Leckey (6)
Newbuildings Primary School, Londonderry

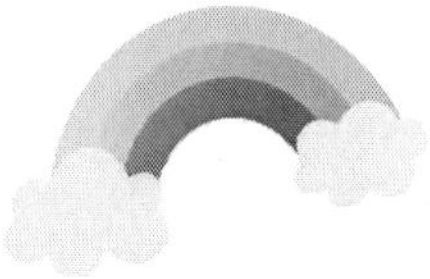

Dinner

D ressed in tomato sauce.
I like ice cream.
N ice and healthy pasta.
N o more vegetables.
E at it all up.
R eheat when cold.

Hope Éirinn Cunningham (5)
Newbuildings Primary School, Londonderry

Henry

H olidays are over.
E veryone's back at school.
N ow hard work begins.
R eading books.
Y es, I love school.

Henry Morrison (5)
Newbuildings Primary School, Londonderry

Farm

F armers are always muddy.
A bull is a daddy cow.
R ams like to eat grass.
M y farm has lots of mud.

Billy Spence (6)
Newbuildings Primary School, Londonderry

Catherine

C oke is my favourite drink
A pples are my favourite fruit
T om is my oldest brother
H orses are beautiful and I love them
E llen is my best friend
R iding horses is fun for me
I like saying my prayers in Mass
N ever eat Brussels sprouts
E aster eggs are delicious.

Catherine Brigit McGinn (8)
St Joseph's Primary School, Bessbrook

Micéal

M y favourite is Saturday
I like football
C ars are my favourite type of vehicle
E very day I go to my granny's
A lways watching movies
L ove dogs.

Micéal McGowan (7)
St Joseph's Primary School, Bessbrook

Ellen

E very day I play with my friends
L ollipops are my favourite sweets
L earning in school is fun
E ach day I ride horses
N ever go behind my horse.

Ellen Rose Murphy (8)
St Joseph's Primary School, Bessbrook

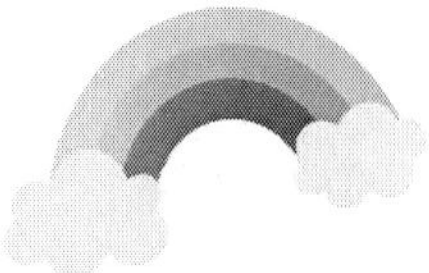

Kevin

K iwi is my favourite food
E aster is my favourite time of year
V ans are my favourite shoes
I like bouncy balls
N ever support Liverpool.

Kevin Wallace (7)
St Joseph's Primary School, Bessbrook

Oisin

O ranges are my favourite fruit
I love igloos
S harks are my favourite animal
I love bananas
N ever support Liverpool!

Oisin Malone (7)
St Joseph's Primary School, Bessbrook

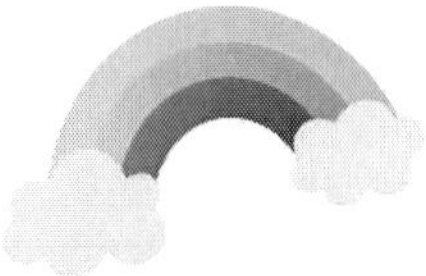

Ryan

R ed is my second favourite colour
Y o-yos are cool
A lways laughing
N eat and tidy always.

Ryan Murphy (7)
St Joseph's Primary School, Bessbrook

Shea

S ometimes silly
H appy all the time
E nergetic, always on the go
A lways laughing.

Shea McComb (7)

St Joseph's Primary School, Bessbrook

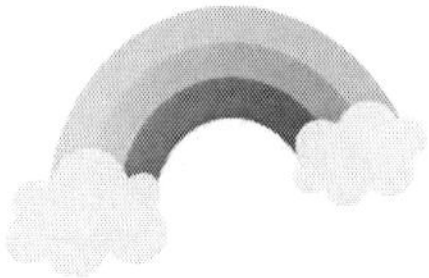

Leo

L unch is my favourite time
E very day I eat cheese
O ranges give me wet fingers.

Leo Hughes (7)
St Joseph's Primary School, Bessbrook

Dearbhla

D ucks are my favourite animals
E very day I play with my friends
A pples are my favourite fruit
R eading is my favourite thing to do
B rown is the colour of my hair
H atchimals are my favourite toy
L .O.L. dolls are my second favourite toy
A lways go to a restaurant.

Dearbhla Bateson (7)
St Mary's Primary School, Portglenone

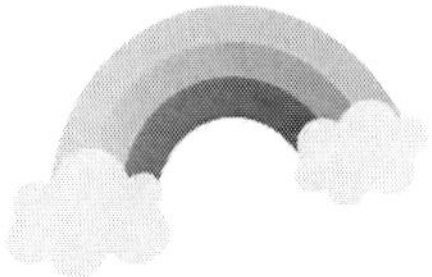

Zuzanna L

Z oos are my favourite places
U nder my favourite blanket
Z ebras are my favourite animals
A lways play with my friend
N utella is my favourite treat
N ever embarrassed
A lways kind to people

L ike to go to the park.

Zuzanna Lewecka (7)
St Mary's Primary School, Portglenone

Rebecca

R unning as fast as I can in a race
E ating a lot of Fruitella
B ees make yummy honey
E veryone is nice to me
C ake is my favourite
C akes and cream are the best
A nimals are my favourite.

Rebecca Fisher (7)
St Mary's Primary School, Portglenone

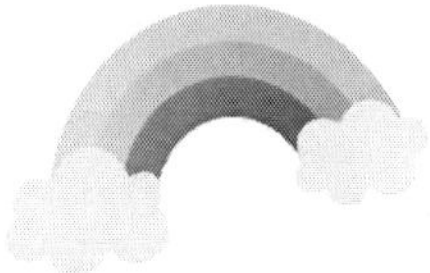

Eimear

E xcellent at art
I love to play with my friends
M y mummy plays camogie with me
E lephants are too big for me
A dorable bunnies are so cute
R ed is my favourite colour.

Eimear Blaney (7)
St Mary's Primary School, Portglenone

Caolan

C runchie bars are my favourite!
A lways making lots of mess
O utside playing with my friends
L ove playing Minecraft
A melon is my favourite fruit
N ice Sunday dinner.

Caolan McCoy (7)
St Mary's Primary School, Portglenone

Jayden

J umping in muddy puddles
A lways loves my mummy
Y o-yos are my favourite thing to play with
D earbhla is my friend
E lectronics are the best
N utella is my favourite.

Jayden Paxton (7)
St Mary's Primary School, Portglenone

Caidán

C aolan and Tomas are my best friends
A lways having fun
I am the best footballer
D rinking hot chocolate
A lways having a chat
N ever giving up.

Caidán Convery (6)
St Mary's Primary School, Portglenone

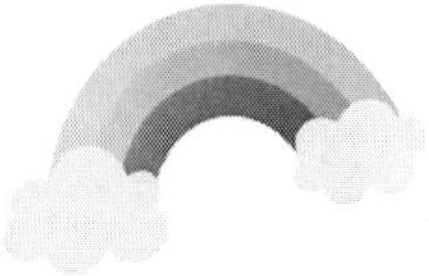

Caitlin

C alm and casual
A lways chilling
I n the garden
T he sun shining
L oving life
I 'm loving the weather
N ever going inside.

Caitlin Dougan (7)
St Mary's Primary School, Portglenone

Katie

K ittens are my favourite animal
A pples are my favourite fruit
T om is my best friend
I ce cream is my favourite treat
E very day I go on my swing.

Katie McCallion (7)

St Mary's Primary School, Portglenone

Naoisha Kelly

N ever giving up
A lways playing
O ut and about
I love reading
S ometimes I shout
H appy every day
A dog is my favourite.

Naoisha Kelly (7)
St Mary's Primary School, Portglenone

Niamh S

N iamh is nice
I love unicorns
A ll my friends are nice
M y mummy is kind to me
H ot hot dogs

S mart little chick.

Niamh Smith (7)
St Mary's Primary School, Portglenone

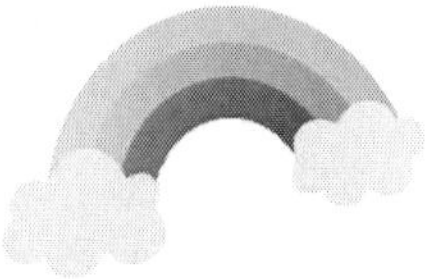

Niamh

N utella is so, so good
I ce cream is so cold
A ll my friends are kind
M y family love me
H ot chocolate is so, so hot!

Niamh Mulholland (7)
St Mary's Primary School, Portglenone

Paula

P rincess of puppies
A lways a good friend
U nicorns are my friend
L ove horses and bunnies
A nd adore my dog, Rosie.

Paula McCann (7)
St Mary's Primary School, Portglenone

Tomás

T he best footballer
O utside in the sun
M aking lots of mess
A lways having a chat
S aturdays are the best.

Tomás Soares (7)
St Mary's Primary School, Portglenone

Jack

J umps everywhere while eating sweets
A lways sharing and caring
C ourageous and brave
K ing of koalas.

Jack Alastair Kearney (8)
St Mary's Primary School, Portglenone

Cody

C hocolate is the best
O ranges and Oreos are yummy
D ogs are kind
Y oghurts, I don't like them!

Cody Graffin (7)
St Mary's Primary School, Portglenone

Ethan

E xcellent I am at soccer
T urtles are my favourite animals
H appy I am because my brother plays with me
A wesome I am at football
N ice I am.

Ethan James Dalzell (7)
St Oliver Plunkett's Primary School, Kilmore

Sean McCann

S ean's favourite fruit are blackberries
E lephants are my favourite animal
A pples are my favourite fruit
N ests I have never seen before.

Sean McCann (7)
St Oliver Plunkett's Primary School, Kilmore

Cadhla

C ats I do not like
A ll day I play
D ogs I like
H orses I want to ride
L ots of fun
A lot of friends I have.

Cadhla Morgan (6)
St Oliver Plunkett's Primary School, Kilmore

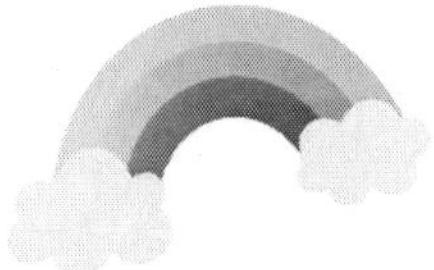

Ollie Lawless

O rchards are beside my house
L ollies, I like
L ions, I like
I have a pet dog and he comes when you fall
E ggs, I like.

Ollie Lawless (6)
St Oliver Plunkett's Primary School, Kilmore

All About Lara Cullen

L asagne is my favourite food at school
A pples are my favourite snack
R ainbows make me so so happy
A rt is my favourite activity.

Lara Cullen (6)

St Oliver Plunkett's Primary School, Kilmore

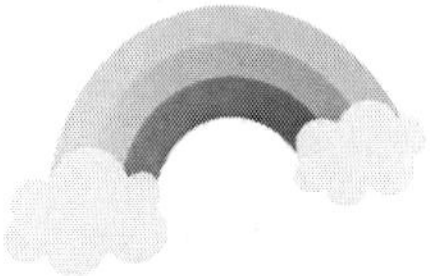

Paul

P igs are my first animal
A pples are my first fruit
U mbrellas keep me dry
L ions are my second favourite animal.

Paul McGrane (6)
St Oliver Plunkett's Primary School, Kilmore

Macie

M cDonald's is tasty
A pples are tasty
C omfy I am sleeping
I ce cream is tasty
E ggs are tasty.

Macie Dunlop (6)
St Oliver Plunkett's Primary School, Kilmore

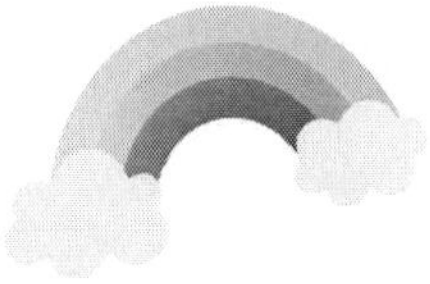

All About Ivy

I love ice cream
V ery good work I can do
Y ellow is my favourite colour

S un is my favourite weather.

Ivy Smyth (6)
St Oliver Plunkett's Primary School, Kilmore

All About Cara

C ormac is my brother and he is big
A rmagh, I live in, it is the best
R ainbows I like
A pples I eat at home.

Cara Murphy (6)
St Oliver Plunkett's Primary School, Kilmore

All About Tara

T igers I don't like
A pples I like for lunch
R abbits are really, really cute
A rmagh I live in.

Tara Donnelly (7)
St Oliver Plunkett's Primary School, Kilmore

Ryan

R abbits are near my house
Y awning I like
A stronauts are cool
N ests I have seen.

Ryan Skeath (7)
St Oliver Plunkett's Primary School, Kilmore

Clodagh

C areful to everybody I know
L ovely to my cat, Bonnie
O reo ice cream is my favourite ice cream
D ays of the week are school days but
weekends aren't
A lice is funny, she is my classmate
G rainne is at my table
H appy with everything I do.

Clodagh Collins (7)
St Patrick's Primary School Ballygalget, Portaferry

Grainne

G ood at being a friend
R ainbows are lovely and are my favourite
A lice is my cousin and I love her
I help my mummy
N ature is my favourite thing outside
N ew toys I get, old toys I give away
E very day I help my friends.

Grainne Birt (7)
St Patrick's Primary School Ballygalget, Portaferry

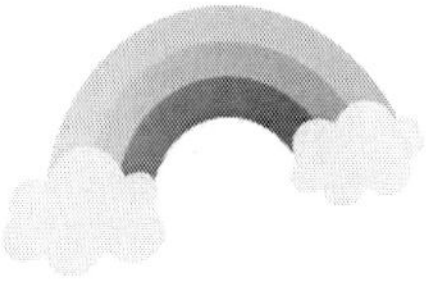

Cormac

C hocolate milk is my favourite drink
O utside, I play hurley
R unning is my favourite sport
M y mummy, daddy and my sister, Mia, are
the best people in the world
A dog is my favourite animal
C hocolate is my favourite food.

Cormac Conlan (8)
St Patrick's Primary School Ballygalget, Portaferry

Kaiden

K ing of football being in net
A pples are my favourite fruit
I 'm nuts, if you hop on a rock you can
drive it
D onal is my best friend
E very day I go to the beach
N ever give up on anything.

Kaiden Mathews (8)
St Patrick's Primary School Ballygalget, Portaferry

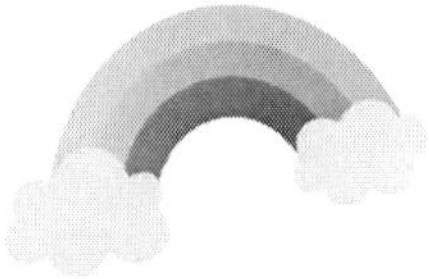

Rosa

R ainbows are my favourite things!
O utside is best because I get to play with my friends
S inging. I love to sing. My favourite singer is Katy Perry
A rtistic. I love art, it's my favourite subject in school!

Rosa McClure (7)
St Patrick's Primary School Ballygalget, Portaferry

Eoin

E very day after school I go outside and play football because it's my favourite sport
O striches are my favourite animals
I like eating pizza
N ew clothes are my favourite thing.

Eoin Gordon (8)
St Patrick's Primary School Ballygalget, Portaferry

Alice

A unicorn is the cutest thing
L uke is my cute and cuddly teddy
I love pancakes, yummy!
C hocolate is my favourite snack
E very day I try my best!

Alice Magee (7)
St Patrick's Primary School Ballygalget, Portaferry

Erin

E very day I like to play with my dolls
R un in the sun is what I like to do outside
I like to eat strawberry ice cream
N ever give up on my work.

Erin Fisher (7)
St Patrick's Primary School Ballygalget, Portaferry

Emily

E lephants are one of my favourite animals
M y favourite thing is art
I like ice skating
L ove chocolate
Y o-yos are my favourite toy.

Emily Clarke (8)
St Patrick's Primary School Ballygalget, Portaferry

Nina

N utella is my favourite chocolate in the world
I love vanilla ice cream
N ecklaces are my favourite jewellery
A mazing at swimming in the pool.

Nina Gordon (8)
St Patrick's Primary School Ballygalget, Portaferry

Paud

P laying hurley is my favourite sport
A mazing at striking the ball
U nicorns are my favourite animal
D ogs can be dirty from rolling in mud.

Paud Braniff (7)
St Patrick's Primary School Ballygalget, Portaferry

Iona

I love ice cream and chocolate
O ranges are my favourite fruit
N uts are my favourite snack
A lion is my favourite animal.

Iona McClements (8)
St Patrick's Primary School Ballygalget, Portaferry

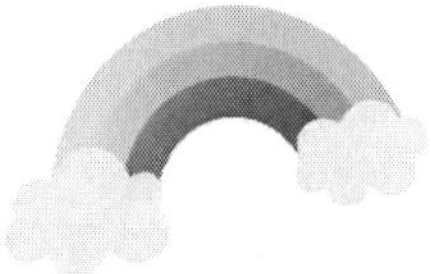

Úna

U nicorns are my favourite animal
N ina is my friend
A mazing at Irish dancing.

Úna Savage (7)
St Patrick's Primary School Ballygalget, Portaferry

Van Dijk

V an Dijk is the best footballer in the world
A footballer has to have good
sportsmanship
N ow Van Dijk is the best player in Liverpool

D o you like Van Dijk?
I know I do. Yes, you must like Van Dijk
J oyful every day to think about Van Dijk
K now to stop wearing Manchester rigs and
wear Liverpool rigs.

Layna-Rae Mooney (7)
St Therese's Primary School, Galliagh

Kelvin

K elvin is my favourite name
E lvis is my elf's name
L ove my mummy and daddy
V ery good at playing football
I love my brother, Theo
N o, I do not like Brussels sprouts.

Kelvin Waterkamp (7)
St Therese's Primary School, Galliagh

Dance

D ancing is my favourite sport
A Feis is very fun
N ever give up in dance
C urry would not be nice before dance
E ggs, bacon and chips would be nice
before dance.

Rebecca Powell (8)
St Therese's Primary School, Galliagh

Family

F amily is the best
A family is special
M y family is inspirational
I love my family with all my heart
L ove everybody
Y ou are the best.

Charli Jessica Brett (8)
St Therese's Primary School, Galliagh

School

S t Therese is the name
C hairs are used for sitting
H ave a good school
O ther children go there
O ne of my friends is Conan
L ove it.

Riley James Michael McDonald (8)
St Therese's Primary School, Galliagh

Aoibhe

A unicorn is so cute
O ranges are so good
I love chocolate
B ikes are fun
H annah is my best friend
E mily is my best friend.

Aoibhe Mary Ramsey (7)
St Therese's Primary School, Galliagh

Games

G ames are fun
A t my birthday I played a game
M inecraft is my favourite game
E ven my daddy plays games
S urvival mode is hard and fun.

Rhys Simpson (8)
St Therese's Primary School, Galliagh

Gaming

G aming is fun!
A nd Fortnite too.
M inecraft a bit.
I like Apex too.
N ights gaming on my Xbox is fun!
G aming is the best.

Colm Harkin (7)
St Therese's Primary School, Galliagh

Kayla

K oalas are my favourite
A mazing to my friends
Y o-yos are my favourite
L ove my mummy lots and lots
A pples are my favourite fruit.

Kayla Coyle (7)
St Therese's Primary School, Galliagh

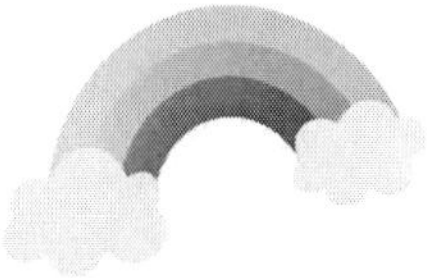

Games

G ames are fun
A game is what you play
M inecraft is good
E very day I play my Xbox
S ometimes my mum tells me to stop.

Tristan Pennock (7)
St Therese's Primary School, Galliagh

Sing

S inging is my favourite hobby
I like listening to Justin Bieber
N othing is better than Katy Perry
G o to choir at school.

Chloe Sweeney (7)
St Therese's Primary School, Galliagh

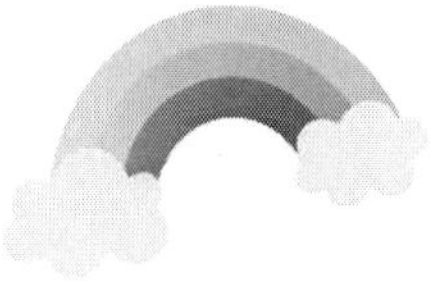

Team

T he best team is Liverpool
E very day Liverpool plays I watch them
A ll my friends watch Liverpool
M y dad likes Liverpool.

Lewis Hargan (7)
St Therese's Primary School, Galliagh

Emily

E mily is my name
M y friend's name is Rebecca
I ce cream is good
L ove my dog
Y ou are fun.

Emily McLaughlin (7)
St Therese's Primary School, Galliagh

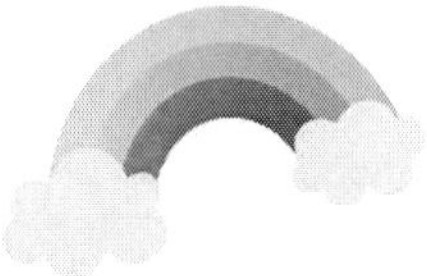

Riley

R eally kind boy
I like chocolate
L ike playing ball
E qual to my friends
Y ellow bike.

Riley Derges (8)
St Therese's Primary School, Galliagh

Cats

C ats are loving and cute
A cat is a good pet
T o me, cats are good animals
S o I like cats.

Dakota Lauren Shields (7)
St Therese's Primary School, Galliagh

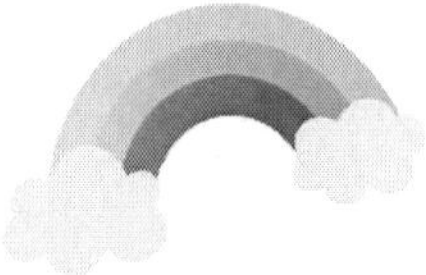

Xbox

X boxes are fun
B oxes are fun
O h my god, this is the best game
X boxes are the best.

Eamonn Christopher McKnight (7)
St Therese's Primary School, Galliagh

Katie

K ind
A good friend
T idy
I like my friend
E very day I play.

Katie-Leigh Burke (7)
St Therese's Primary School, Galliagh

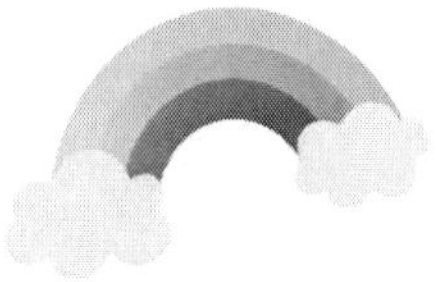

Fun

F ire is not fun
U p on the trampoline is fun
N ever stop having fun.

Conan John McCoy (8)
St Therese's Primary School, Galliagh

Fun

F ootball is the best
U p in the sky when I jump
N erf guns are fun.

James Ferry (7)
St Therese's Primary School, Galliagh

YoungWriters
Est. 1991

Young Writers Information

We hope you have enjoyed reading this book – and that you will continue to in the coming years.

If you're a young writer who enjoys reading and creative writing, or the parent of an enthusiastic poet or story writer, do visit our website **www.youngwriters.co.uk**. Here you will find free competitions, workshops and games, as well as recommended reads, a poetry glossary and our blog. There's lots to keep budding writers motivated to write!

If you would like to order further copies of this book, or any of our other titles, then please give us a call or order via your online account.

Young Writers
Remus House
Coltsfoot Drive
Peterborough
PE2 9BF
(01733) 890066
info@youngwriters.co.uk

Join in the conversation!
Tips, news, giveaways and much more!

YoungWritersUK

@YoungWritersCW